The Tobermory Shipwrecks

By Rick Salen

drawings by Jack Salen

Published by
The Mariner Chart Shop
Tobermory

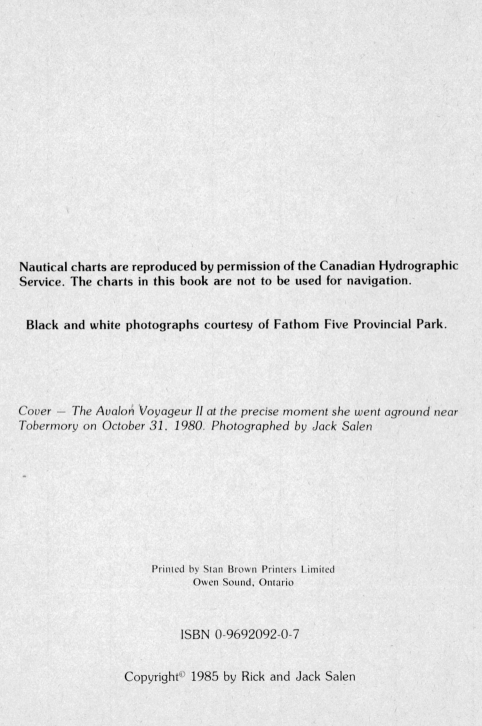

Nautical charts are reproduced by permission of the Canadian Hydrographic Service. The charts in this book are not to be used for navigation.

Black and white photographs courtesy of Fathom Five Provincial Park.

Cover — The Avalon Voyageur II at the precise moment she went aground near Tobermory on October 31, 1980. Photographed by Jack Salen

Printed by Stan Brown Printers Limited
Owen Sound, Ontario

ISBN 0-9692092-0-7

printed in Canada

Table of Contents

Charts

Acknowledgements

Special thanks to the following people who were most helpful in providing information and materials used in this book.

Stan McClellan
Jack Youngblut
Dr. George Harpur
Capt. Hank and Thelma Buitendyk
Danny Beemer
Don McIver

my wife Lindsey for her assistance.

Introduction

The Tobermory shipwrecks provide a rare and important link to our nineteenth century Great Lakes heritage. They remain in tribute to the skills of the wooden ship-builders and in testimony of the hardships and challenges faced by the crews.

To understand why there are so many shipwrecks near Tobermory one must look at the geography of the area. At Tobermory, the Niagara Escarpment, a ridge of rock running through Southern Ontario, submerges and reappears 30 miles to the north as Manitoulin Island. In between, the escarpment re-emerges in the form of islands and shoals, all obstacles to the ships sailing between Lake Huron and Georgian Bay. Three channels near Tobermory offer passage. They include the four-mile wide Main Channel between Cove and Yeo Islands, the Devil Island Channel between Cove and Russel, just 1200 feet wide in places and the Cape Hurd Channel between Russel Island and the mainland. This is the most treacherous of the three being less than 900 feet wide in several places. Both the Devil Island and Cape Hurd Channels are bordered by large areas of shoal, rising quickly out of the depths to within a few feet of the surface. Passage through these channels could be a feat of considerable challenge when aboard a schooner relying on wind-power alone, or aboard a steamer towing one or two barges.

Ship traffic around Tobermory began in earnest during the 1850's. Traffic inbound was mainly schooners from the lower lakes bringing in supplies to the developing lumber towns around Georgian Bay. Outbound schooners carried the lumber to the growing urban centers of the United States and Canada. During the 1860's grain from the American Midwest was being shipped to Collingwood, which was connected to the eastern markets by rail. The railroad opened the ports of Owen Sound and Midland during the 1880's.

The typical Great Lakes schooner of the nineteenth century was two or three-masted and rigged in either a topsail or fore and aft configuration. Most were equipped with a large centerboard that reduced drift, added stability and when raised allowed them to enter shallow harbours. The Canadian-built schooners were usually shorter than the American vessels, thus allowing them passage through the Welland Canal with its maximum lock length of 140 feet. Frames and planking were usually white oak. The masts of white pine were two to four feet thick at deck level and soared 80 to 100 feet above it. The mast backstays were usually wire and the running-gear was of hemp or manilla. The schooners were crewed with between five and ten men each.

By 1890, black coal-soot spewing from the stacks of steamers was rapidly replacing the sight of canvas passing by the Tobermory islands. Many of the steamers were coasters, carrying passengers and general wares to the towns and hamlets around Georgian Bay.

By this time the aids to navigation had been greatly improved due to the increasing number of shipwrecks. Between 1884 and 1888, Captain J. G. Boulton and crew of the steamer Bayfield performed the first complete survey of Georgian Bay. Three lighthouses were erected near Tobermory during the second half of the nineteenth century; Cove Island in 1858, Big Tub in 1885 and Flowerpot in 1897. As a result of these navigational improvements the frequency of shipwrecks declined. Even today however, the rock shoals, high winds, fog and mechanical failure continue to add to the list of Tobermory shipwrecks.

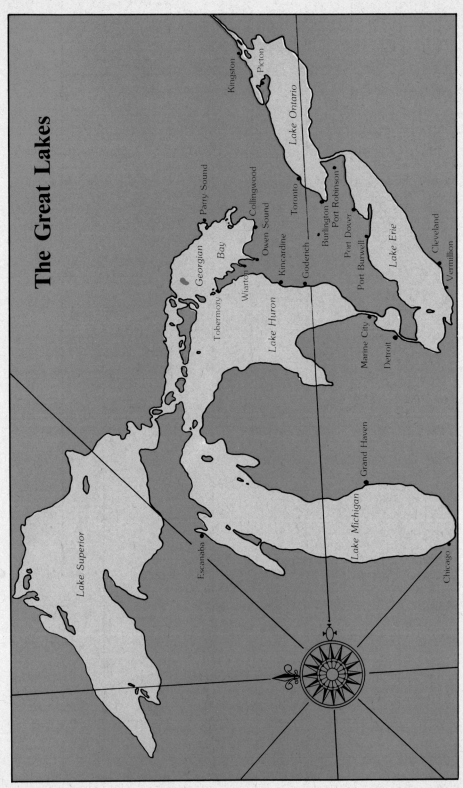

The Great Lakes

Lake Superior

Escanaba

Lake Michigan

Grand Haven

Chicago

Tobermory

Georgian Bay

Parry Sound

Collingwood

Owen Sound

Wiarton

Lake Huron

Kincardine

Godereich

Marine City

Detroit

Burlington

Port Robinson

Port Dover

Port Burwell

Lake Erie

Cleveland

Vermillion

Toronto

Kingston

Picton

Lake Ontario

The Maritime History of Tobermory

The lives and activities of Tobermory's residents have always centered around boats and the two, fine harbours of Big Tub and Little Tub. Its strategic location has made Tobermory a port of refuge for canoe, mackinaw boat, schooner, steamer and yacht. The harbours have also provided an ideal base of operations to fleets of fishing tugs, the Manitoulin ferries, guide boats, dive tugs and tour boats.

Tobermory's harbours and the waters off-shore were partially surveyed in 1815 by the British Navy Admiral William Fitwilliam Owen aboard the schooner Huron. In 1818 his successor, Lieutenant Henry Bayfield, completed the task aboard the vessels Troughton and Ramsden. Bayfield's assistant was midshipman Philip E. Collins, and so, on Bayfield's chart of 1822 Tobermory was named Collins Harbour. However, by 1850 it was being called Tobermory by the Scottish immigrants from the Goderich area who had begun fishing around the tip of the Bruce Peninsula. They were no doubt reminded of Tobermory, Scotland.

Tobermory's first permanent settler, Charles Earl, arrived with his family aboard the schooner Nee-Chee in 1871. Big Tub Harbour was already in heavy use by vessels seeking shelter so Earl fastened a lantern atop a tree to guide them in. Big Tub Lighthouse was built in 1885 and Earl was appointed keeper. In 1881 iron rings and hooks, which can still be seen, were attached to the shoreline of Big Tub to aid mooring vessels.

By the time Charles Earl arrived, the fishermen from the Goderich and Southampton areas had been joined by fishermen from the Meaford area. Both groups fished from small, open centerboard sailboats but it seems the Georgian Bay preferred the traditional, double-ended Mackinaw boat over the square sterned version used by the Lake Huron men. Both groups maintained fishing stations on nearby islands including Flowerpot and Halfmoon, where they salted and barreled their catches of laketrout. During the 1880's the fishing stations moved to Tobermory and the steam fish-tug made its appearance.

Both harbours were bustling during the late 1880's and 90's. Coastal steamers like the Telegram, J. H. Jones. and City of Grand Rapids called regularly, bringing new settlers and supplies, and leaving with the ice-packed catches of fish, or with loads of Bruce Peninsula pine.

Three sawmills were in operation around Little Tub Harbour by 1900. Booms of logs cut from the then plentiful forests of the northern Bruce Peninsula were towed by steam tugs to Tobermory where they were square-sawn and then loaded onto schooners and steamers bound for the lower lakes.

Logging activity declined during the 1920's and fishing again became the mainstay of the local economy. By 1930 there were fifteen steam tugs operating out of Tobermory but by the end of the decade over-fishing and the lamprey eel caused the catches to dwindle. Presently there are five fishing boats in Tobermory bringing in moderate catches of whitefish and chub.

During the 1930's, the famous Tobermory fleet of guide boats began to develop. The 30 to 50-foot-long wooden cabin cruisers carried hunters and fishermen on week-long trips to the north-shore of Georgian Bay and the North Channel above Manitoulin Island. At the height of their popularity in the late 40's there were 25 such boats in Tobermory. Almost all were built locally by their owners.

A very important chapter of Tobermory's maritime history concerns the Tobermory to Manitoulin Island ferry service. It began operations in 1930 with the 90-foot-long Kagawong. She ran one trip a day carrying up to eight cars. Two years later the 125-foot Normac took over and stayed on the run until 1963. ° The 200-foot, 50-car Norisle, built at Collingwood ran from 1946 to 1974. The Norgoma carried 38 vehicles and worked with the Norisle from 1962 to 1974 when they were both replaced by the 140-car Chi-Cheemaun. The 365-foot-long Chi-Cheemaun (meaning Big Canoe in Ojibway), was also built at Collingwood.

Vessels from Tobermory have always been quick to aid others in distress. While reading the following accounts of shipwrecks you will notice that the crews of the stricken vessels were often rescued by a Tobermory tug. Since 1978 most of this duty has been assumed by the Canadian Coast Guard's 44-foot search and rescue vessel 108.

Whether you are scuba-diving, riding aboard a tour-boat, or just watching the fish-tugs and yachts come and go, Tobermory offers an exceptional opportunity to see and experience our Great Lakes maritime heritage, past and present.

Photo Credit by J.James & Daughters

°The Normac became Captain John's floating restaurant in Toronto. Her career ended when she was rammed and sunk by a Toronto Island ferry.

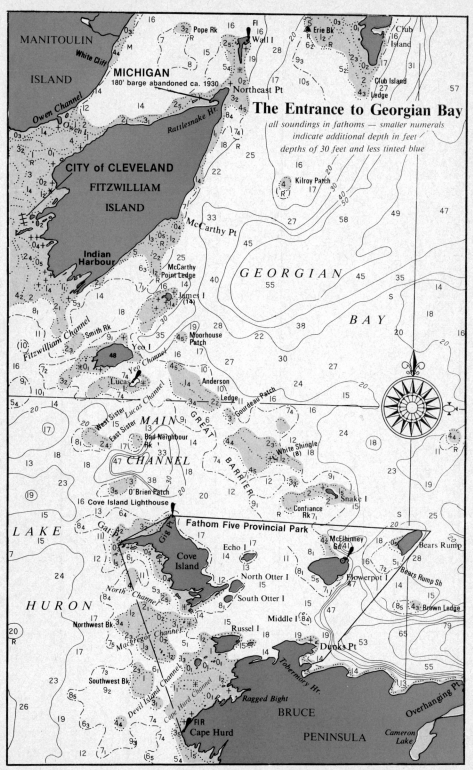

The Entrance to Georgian Bay

*all soundings in fathoms — smaller numerals
indicate additional depth in feet
depths of 30 feet and less tinted blue*

MANITOULIN

ISLAND

White Cliff

Owen Channel

MICHIGAN
180' barge abandoned ca. 1930

Northeast Pt

Pope Rk

Wall I

Erie Bk

Club
Island

Club Island
Ledge

Rattlesnake Hr.

CITY of CLEVELAND

FITZWILLIAM

ISLAND

Indian
Harbour

McCarthy Pt

Kilroy Patch

GEORGIAN

BAY

McCarthy
Point Ledge

James I
(14)

Fitzwilliam Channel

Smith Rk

Yeo I

Moorhouse
Patch

Yeo Channel

Lucas

Anderson
Ledge

Gourdeau Patch

West Sister

East Sister

MAIN

Lucas Channel

Bad Neighbour
Rk

GREAT

White Shingle
(8)

Snake I

CHANNEL

BARRIER

O'Brien Patch

Confiance
Rk

Cove Island Lighthouse

Fathom Five Provincial Park

LAKE

Gat

Gig Pt

Echo I

McElhinney
Gd (4)

Bears Rump

Cove
Island

North Otter I

Flowerpot I

Bears Rump Sh

HURON

North Channel

South Otter I

Brown Ledge

Northwest Bk

Macgregor Channel

Russel I

Middle I

Dunks Pt

Southwest Bk

Devil Island Channel

Cape Hurd Channel

Ragged Bight

BRUCE

Overhanging Pt

FIR
Cape Hurd

PENINSULA

Cameron
Lake

9

Fathom Five Provincial Park

Fathom Five Provincial Park is one of 112 operating provincial parks in the Province of Ontario. It is administered by the Parks and Recreation Branch of the Ontario Ministry of Natural Resources and is currently the only one in the system with the primary emphasis on the aquatic environment and the associated resources. The park consists of two major components, a 142 hectare land base portion is as yet undeveloped. The water base portion encompasses about 72 square kilometres of lake bed in Lake Huron and Georgian Bay. While the park boundaries embrace the group of islands historically known as the Cape Hurd Islands, none of them are a part of Fathom Five Park. Many of the islands are owned by the Federal Government and in fact form a part of Georgian Bay Islands National Park.

Protection of the resources, both natural and historical, is a primary concern of the park program. Biological and geological features provide some of the areas finest natural scenic attractions. Historical evidence comes alive both above and below the water surface. Cove Island Light Station, one of the oldest on the Upper Great Lakes (1856), marks the northern park boundary. Research has indicated that at least twenty six vessels of all types have been lost within the park limits. To date, some twenty have been located and most are an important part of the diving and tour boat visitor's agenda.

Sport diving is a major activity in the park and divers are reminded that several park regulations are applicable to their sport. Safe diving practices are encouraged and monitored and some requirements are as follows: use of a recognized dive flag is mandatory and all diving must take place in designated areas only. Most harbour areas and vessel traffic lanes are closed to diving. Removal of any natural or historical material is strictly prohibited and charges could result from any violation of this regulation. Each diver is required, once annually, on the first visit of the season, to register prior to any diving within the park limits. The Park Visitor Centre is open daily from early May until late October and all visitors are encouraged to drop in and obtain information designed to provide a safe and enjoyable visit to the park.

Regular patrols are carried out in the radio equipped vessel. Staff and volunteers are trained and capable of dealing with any emergency and have a thorough knowledge of the park and its resources. These friendly people can assist you with site locations, re: weather conditions or answer specific questions about the area. In addition, the Friends of Fathom Five Park is a co-operating association dedicated to assisting the park and its programs and their efforts are also aimed at providing general and specific information to further enhance your visit.

For further information contact the Park Superintendent, Fathom Five Provinicial Park, Tobermory, Ontario, N0H 2R0

Diving Safety in Tobermory

The following was provided by Dr. George Harpur.

The Tobermory Hyperbaric Facility is an integral part of the community health clinic and is situated 1.6 kilometers south of Little Tub Harbour on the west side of Highway 6. The facility was installed in 1976 with a grant from the Ministry of Natural Resources and the assistance of many divers and dive clubs.

The clinic physicians are all divers and most are diving instructors. The chamber crew consists of individuals who have been especially trained for this function. Some of this staff is full time but most are part time.

The chief activity of the chamber since its installation has been student diver instruction. A program of tours, lectures, and chamber dives has been provided at modest cost for about 1000 divers per year. This program has been well received and is a successful contribution to the excellent safety record diving enjoys in Tobermory.

Over 30,000 dives are made each year in Tobermory and the number grows steadily each season. Despite these numbers the incidence of serious accidents has been steadily declining and is now at a very low level, considerably below the risk for the drive up from the population centres to the south. This trend is a reflection of many things; improved equipment, better instruction, better attitudes and modification in techniques which reflect new knowledge. The well-organized support structures and the presence of the chamber all enhance this basic safety for divers in Tobermory. Well trained Fathom Five park staff with radio communication and good boats in co-operation with the Ontario Provincial Police and the volunteer ambulance service respond promptly to emergencies. Rapid evacuation combined with the prompt use of medical facilities and the chamber has resulted in a very favourable outcome in the majority of cases.

In the interests of diving safety and in an attempt to maintain and improve this record, the following should be considered by all divers coming to this area.

Each diver has a responsibility to ensure that they are fit for any given dive. Fitness to dive involves being physically fit. Every year we have to treat people who have an accident which should have precluded diving at all. Temporary problems due to colds shouldn't be ignored, they can have serious consequences.

The diver must be psychologically fit and in Tobermory this means relaxed and comfortable enough to cope with the added stress of cold water.

The diver must be intellectually fit. They must know how to handle problems such as regulator freeze-up, how to dive plan properly and be familiar with emergency procedures and resources in the area.

Finally, equipment and training must be appropriate to the dive. Inadequate protection from the cold adds to stress. A small CO_2 vest may not get you to the surface from greater than 50-60 feet in an emergency.

All divers must be prepared to cope with an emergency if it arrives. The following is a brief outline of some of the important considerations to be remembered.

Prevention is always best and involves dive planning and diver fitness. If you run out of air underwater an alternative air supply is always nice and the best way to handle this situation. If an out of air ascent is made, remember to keep the regulator in your mouth and attempt to breath in and out continuously. If you are deeper than 40 feet or have any doubt about your ability to reach the surface, inflate your vest. Remember, unconsciousness comes on without warning.

If you are faced with a diving accident the most serious problem you may have to deal with is lack of respiration and heart beat so Cardio-Pulmonary-Resuscitation training is essential. If support to respiration or circulation is necessary, Artificial Respiration or Cardio-Pulmonary-Resuscitation should be started promptly. Near drowning is the commonest cause and in divers is usually secondary to air embolism so the head-down, hip and feet elevated at 15 degree position should be used if possible. This position should always be used for the victim of any diving accident if air embolism is suspected. Remember, look out for vomiting and be prepared to roll the victim onto one side, and clear the air-way immediately. Oxygen and resuscitation are not necessary to save life and their use should be left to experienced people at this stage.

Conscious victims with pain, confusion or any symptom suggesting injury should be kept warm, reassured, and transported to the clinic for examination. Pain in the ears and sinuses caused by difficulty with clearing is not an urgent or serious condition but may require treatment if severe. If available, oxygen can be used with conscious patients and may confer some benefits if the trip in is a long one.

In all cases of accident as much information about the event as can be collected should be sent in with the victim. Of particular importance are, depth of the dive, time and onset of symptoms relative to the dive, initial complaint or difficulty, and subsequent changes for better or worse. The chamber should be contacted as soon as possible via radio or telephone with details of the victims condition eg. level of consciousness, breathing, heartbeat, and other responses. The chamber will be able to advise regarding treatment and transport and can arrange for ambulance and medical response.

This brief outline is intended only to serve as a reminder of some of the more important points of managing diving injuries. Every diver should review his basic diving first-aid at least annually, it's part of being fit to dive.

You are invited to drop by the hyperbaric facility between 9am and 5pm any day for a social visit. Safe diving.

Contact numbers for information or accident reporting.
Fathom Five Provincial Park
— phone 596-2503, or call on VHF radio channel 16.
Ontario Provincial Police
— phone 596-2426, or call on VHF radio channel 16.
Tobermory Hyperbaric Facilities
— phone 596-2306, out of hours 596-2305.
Wiarton Coast Guard Radio and the Tobermory Canadian Coast Guard Station both monitor VHF channel 16.

Little Tub Harbour c. 1906

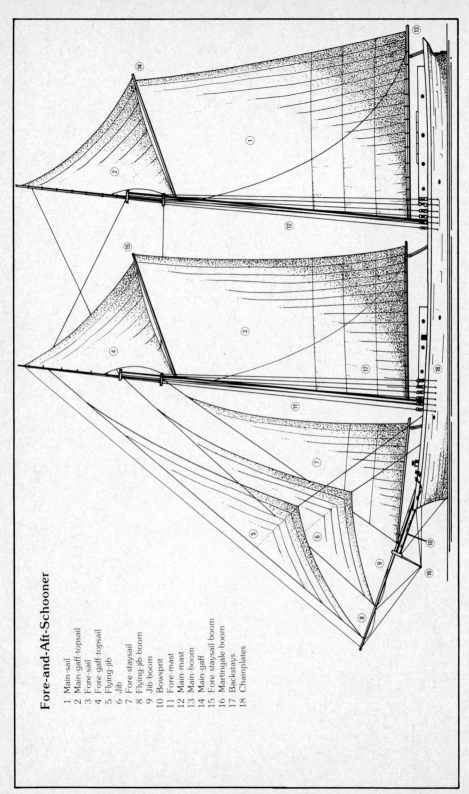

Fore-and-Aft-Schooner

1 Main-sail
2 Main-gaff-topsail
3 Fore-sail
4 Fore-gaff-topsail
5 Flying-jib
6 Jib
7 Fore staysail
8 Flying-jib-boom
9 Jib-boom
10 Bowsprit
11 Fore-mast
12 Main-mast
13 Main-boom
14 Main-gaff
15 Fore staysail-boom
16 Martingale-boom
17 Backstays
18 Chainplates

Topsail-Schooner

1 Main-sail
2 Gaff topsail
3 Main-topmast-staysail
4 Fore-sail
5 Top-sail
6 Topgallant-sail
7 Flying jib
8 Outer-jib
9 Inner-jib
10 Fore-staysail
11 Jib-boom
12 Bow-sprit
13 Martingale boom
14 Bobstay
15 Fore-mast
16 Main-mast
17 Main boom
18 Main gaff
19 Fore yard
20 Backstays
21 Chainplates

Little Tub Harbour c. 1912

Little Tub Harbour

photo by Jack Salen

Fore-Aft Cross Section of a Two-Masted-Schooner — circa 1850

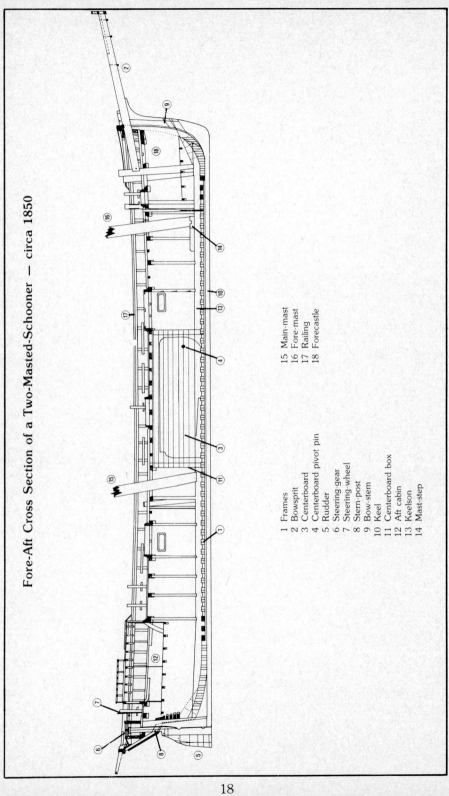

1 Frames
2 Bowsprit
3 Centerboard
4 Centerboard pivot pin
5 Rudder
6 Steering-gear
7 Steering-wheel
8 Stern-post
9 Bow-stem
10 Keel
11 Centerboard box
12 Aft cabin
13 Keelson
14 Mast-step

15 Main-mast
16 Fore-mast
17 Railing
18 Forecastle

Deck Plan of a Two-Masted-Schooner — circa 1850

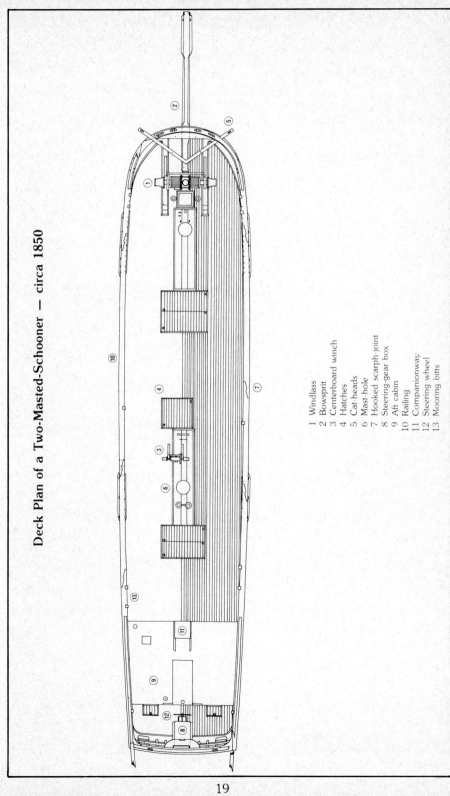

1 Windlass
2 Bowsprit
3 Centerboard winch
4 Hatches
5 Cat-heads
6 Mast-hole
7 Hooked scarph-joint
8 Steering-gear box
9 Aft cabin
10 Railing
11 Companionway
12 Steering wheel
13 Mooring bitts

The windlass of the schooner Sweepstakes

The steamer City of Grand Rapids

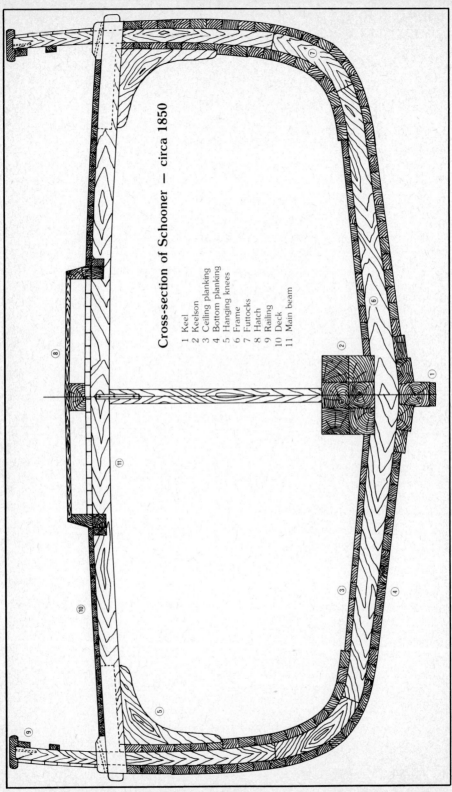

Cross-section of Schooner – circa 1850

1 Keel
2 Keelson
3 Ceiling planking
4 Bottom planking
5 Hanging knees
6 Frame
7 Futtocks
8 Hatch
9 Railing
10 Deck
11 Main beam

Sweepstakes

Gross Tonnage	— 218	Type	— Two-masted schooner
Length	— 120'	Built	— Burlington, Ontario
Breadth	— 23'		1867, by Melancthon
Depth of hold	— 10'		Simpson

The Disaster

In August 1885, the Sweepstakes was stranded on the Cove Island Shoreline. She was pulled off shortly afterwards by the tug Jessie and towed to the head of Big Tub Harbour. She had been badly damaged and sank before repairs could be made. Her cargo of coal was salvaged after she sank.

The Wreck Today

The nearly intact hull of the Sweepstakes is in 20 feet of water and located approximately 50 yards from the head of Big Tub Harbour. A mooring buoy is just east of the wreck. Although deteriorating a little more each year, the Sweepstakes is one of the best preserved nineteenth-century Great Lakes schooners to be found. The bow area is the most interesting with a portion of the starboard railing still intact and the windlass, located on the forward deck. Draught markings carved into the bow-stem are still visable. The two-foot diameter holes through the deck indicate the size and location of the masts. Located amidships, the centerboard box with the centerboard inside, extends from keel to deck. The aft-deck of the Sweepstakes has collapsed and the stern-post now lies on the bottom.

Caution is advised when entering the hull as the Sweepstake's sides and deck are weakening. Repair work has been done by Fathom Five Provincial Park to keep the deck from collapsing.

This site is visited by several glass-bottom tour boats. Because of their restricted manoeuverability and limited visibility it is suggested that you move off the wrecks while the boats are in the area.

The Sweepstakes and the City of Grand Rapids are accessible by boat or by a 400-yard swim from the Big Tub Lodge docks. The land surrounding the head of Big Tub is private.

The stern of the tug Alice G.

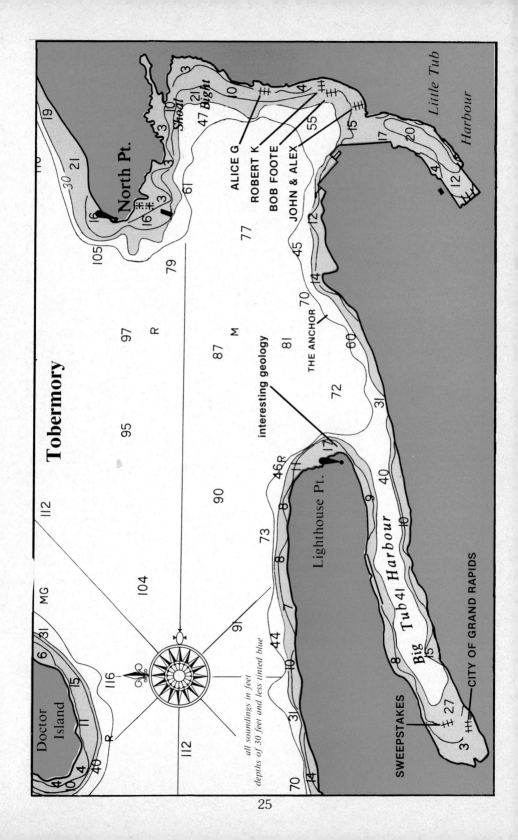

Tobermory

Doctor Island

North Pt.

Shoal

Bight

ALICE G
ROBERT K
BOB FOOTE
JOHN & ALEX

THE ANCHOR

interesting geology

Lighthouse Pt.

Little Tub

Harbour

Big Tub 41 *Harbour*

SWEEPSTAKES

CITY OF GRAND RAPIDS

all soundings in feet
depths of 30 feet and less tinted blue

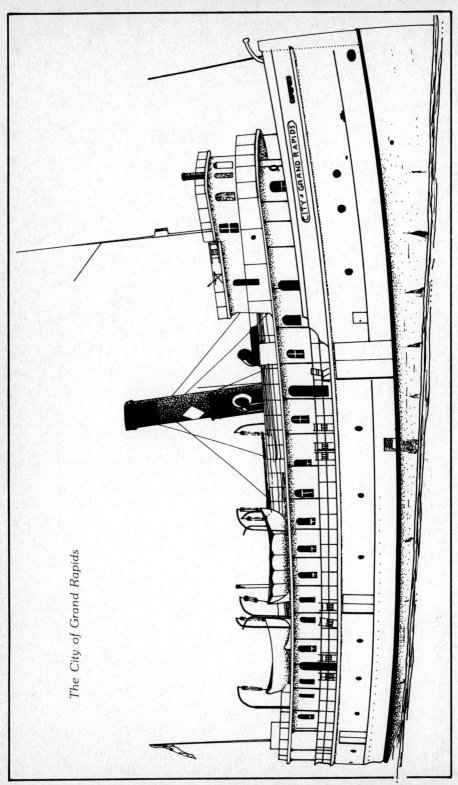

The City of Grand Rapids

City of Grand Rapids

Gross tonnage	— 336	Type	— Propeller coastal steamer
Length	— 122'	Built	— Grand Haven, Michigan
Breadth	— 25'		1879
Depth of hold	— 9'		

The Disaster

The City of Grand Rapids was a double-decked steamer working the coastal trade between Owen Sound and the villages of Manitoulin Island and the Bruce Peninsula. On Oct. 29, 1907, fire broke out aboard the Grand Rapids while docked in Little Tub Harbour. Under the command of Captain Alex Craigie, the tug Clucas took the burning vessel in tow. Just beyond the harbour entrance the tow line burned and the Grand Rapids began to drift down into Big Tub Harbour. She came to rest on the sand bottom at the head of the harbour where she burned to the waterline, rolled to starboard and sank.

The Wreck Today

The City of Grand Rapids lies in less than 10 feet of water and is located 100 feet off the bow of the Sweepstakes. The bottom of the hull is intact from stern to bow, although the hold is almost entirely filled with silt and debris. The port side runs just beneath the surface. The steam engine crankshaft, parts of the boiler, propeller shaft and shaft coupling are present. The rudder and propeller from the Grand Rapids are on display outside the Tobermory and St. Edmunds Township Museum on Highway 6.

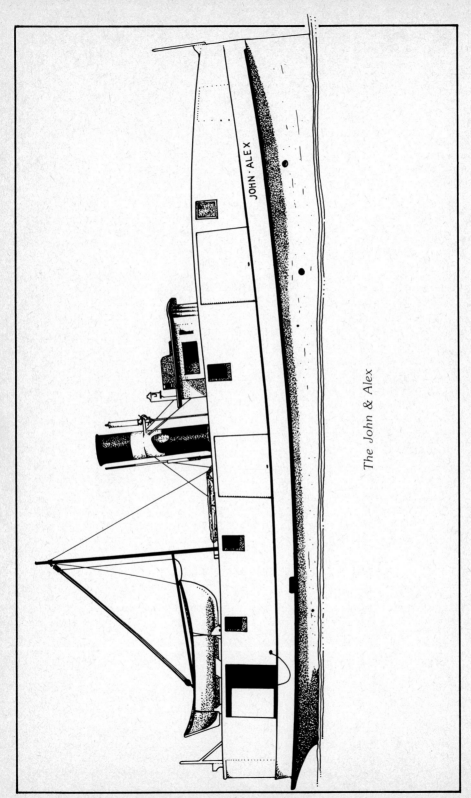

The John & Alex

John & Alex

Gross Tonnage	— 40	Type — Steam fishing tug	
Length	— 59'	Built — Port Dover, Ontario	
Breadth	— 16'		1924, by Charles Percy
Depth of hold	— 7'		Ryerse

The Disaster

The John & Alex joined the Tobermory fishing fleet in 1934. Although built of wood, the John & Alex looked very similar to the steel fish tugs presently fishing out of Tobermory. Her full turtle, or deck covering, was a new innovation as previous fishing tugs were open on deck except for a small wheelhouse situated amidships.

In the early hours of Dec. 6, 1947 fire broke out aboard the John & Alex which was docked in Little Tub Harbour. The vessels nearby were endangered and the burning tug was towed away from them by Audrey Coultis and released at the harbour's mouth. She drifted onto the rocks near Lee Brother's fish shed and burned to the waterline. The John & Alex was owned by W. W. Ransbury at the time and valued at $15,000.

The Wreck Today

The wreck of the John & Alex lies just east of the entrance to Little Tub Harbour. The largest piece of wreckage is a 50-foot-long section of the bottom of the hull. The stern is awash and the forward portion is in 15 feet of water. The stern-tube, engine-bed and the concrete ballast between the frames are the only items of interest on this section. Further east, in 20 to 25 feet of water are smaller sections of the sides and keel.

Bob Foote

Type — Steam fishing tug

The Disaster

The events that led to the wreck of the Bob Foote remain a mystery. We do know that she sank in 1905.

The Wreck Today

The wreckage is in depths of 20 to 25 feet and is located 50 feet south-west of the Robert K. The wreckage measures 56 feet long and 30 feet wide. Both the port and starboard sides have collapsed and the deck has fallen onto the bottom of the hull. The bow stem rises gracefully above the north end of the wreck. Wooden mooring-bitts once used to secure the dock lines are one item of interest.

The remains of two, large, wooden cribs, connected to each other by heavy chain and iron rods, are located just west of the Bob Foote wreckage. They may be part of an old launching slip.

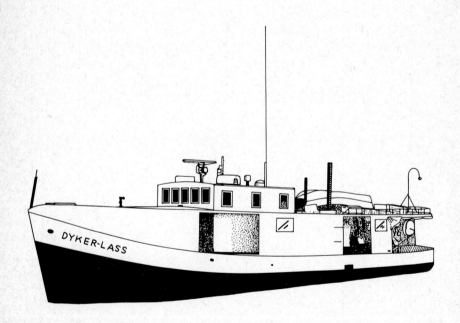

The tug Crawford at Wiarton c. 1915

Robert K

Gross Tonnage	— 56	Type	— Steam fishing tug
Length	— 68'	Built	— Port Dover, Ontario
Breadth	— 17'		1917
Depth of hold	— 7'		by J.E. Paasch

The Disaster
The Robert K., owned by Golden's Fishery was destroyed by fire in 1935.

The Wreck Today
The wreck of the Robert K. is located close to shore directly off the shoreline access in front of the Grandview Motel. The largest piece of wreckage is a 55-foot-long section of the bottom of the hull and keel. A portion of the port side and a section of the stern lie alongside.

Alice G.

Length   — 67'

Type — Steam fishing tug
Built — Collingwood, Ontario

The Disaster

In November 1927, gale-force winds tore the Alice G. from her berth in Little Tub Harbour. The tug was boarded but rammed against the rocky shoreline below North Point before the engine could be fired.

The Wreck Today

The nearly intact wreck of the Alice G. is located 100 yards north of the wreck of the Robert K. It is in 20 feet of water and 50 feet from shore. A mooring buoy is located just west of the wreck.

The steam-engine, boiler, driveshaft and propeller are all intact. The after-deck has collapsed but the stern railing still follows the gracefully curving lines of the fantail stern. The smoke funnel lies on the bottom beneath the starboard side.

China

Gross tonnage	— 319	Type — schooner	
Length	— 137'	Built — Port Robinson, Ontario	
Breadth	— 23'	1863 by	
Depth of hold	— 11'	J. & J. E. Abbey	

The Disaster

In November 1883, the China was sailing up the Cape Hurd Channel destined for Parry Sound where a load of lumber was waiting. With visibility reduced by a snow-squall the China strayed off-course and ran onto the treacherous reef that now bears her name. She was abandoned and broke up during the winter.

The Wreck Today

The wreck of the China is located very close to shore approximately 150 yards south-west of Wreck Point. It is in less than 10 feet of water. All that remains is a 70-foot-long section of the hull bottom including the lower part of the center-board box. The China's rudder lies in 10 feet of water between the wreck and Wreck Point.

Coal barge in Big Tub Harbour c. 1920

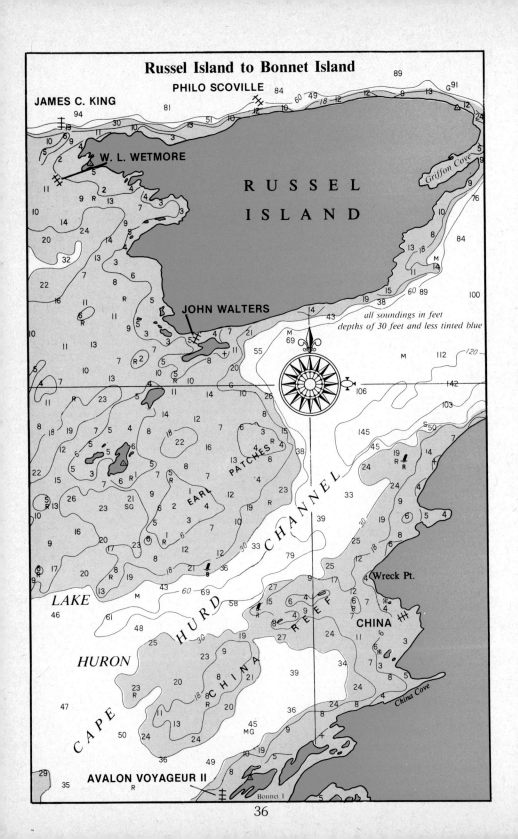

Russel Island to Bonnet Island

36

Avalon Voyageur II

Gross tonnage	— 380	Type	— propellor coastal freighter
Length	— 135'	Built	— Clarenville, Newfoundland
Breadth	— 30'		1947 by
			Clarenville Shipyards

The Disaster

The Avalon Voyageur was the last of ten similar vessels, known as the Splinter Fleet, to be built at the Clarenville Shipyards.* They were a type of vessel called Island Traders, supplying the coastal towns of Newfoundland and Labrador. They also travelled to Nova Scotia, Greenland, the Altantic Seaboard and the West Indies carrying cargos of timber, coal, salted cod and rum.

The Avalon was brought to Toronto in the early 1970's by Art Scott, who used her to house crew members from his tug boat operation. She fell victim to vandals and disrepair until 1978 when purchased by Captain Hank and Thelma Buitendyk. Following a year of repair and renovations the Avalon opened up as a seafood restaurant in Kincardine, Ontario. In the fall of 1980 it was decided to move the Avalon to Owen Sound.

The morning of Oct. 31 was calm when the Avalon left Kincardine harbour under the power of her own 400-horsepower Vivian diesel. As she chugged northward along the coast of the Bruce Peninsula the westerly winds increased to gale force. At the entrance to the Cape Hurd Channel the waterpump belt broke, causing the engine to overheat. An anchor was dropped and Captain Buitendyk and the five crewmembers were rescued from the heavily rolling Avalon by the Tobermory tug W. A. Spears. Shortly afterwards the anchor began to drag and the Avalon drifted up the Cape Hurd Channel until grounding heavily upon a rock ledge off Bonnet Island. The waves continued to pound against her port side until she was firmly entrenched among the rocks. When it calmed, all equipment and furnishings were removed and loaded onto several assisting Tobermory tugs. A concerted effort by the tugs failed in a bid to dislodge the Avalon. She remained relatively intact, albeit listing heavily to port, until Feb. 1982 when vandals set fire to her, gutting the hull.

The Wreck Today

The Avalon lies in less than 15 feet of water just off the west tip of Bonnet Island near Hay Bay. She is lying in a south to north line with her bow pointing north. The hull bottom and lower portion of the starboard side are intact from stern to bow. The top of the engine is awash and the reverse gear, shaft-coupling and shaft are all present. The frames of the Avalon are eight by eight inch oak and the planking is fir and birch. The Avalon is a very good shallow water dive and provides some interesting photography. At times there is a fairly strong current at this location.

---

* The Avalon Voyageur was originally named the Twillingate.

John Walters

Gross tonnage	— 176	Type	— Two-masted schooner
Length	— 108'	Built	— Picton, Ontario
Breadth	— 23'		1852
Depth of hold	— 8'		by George Thurston

The Disaster

The circumstance of the disaster is not known. One can only assume that she ran into trouble while attempting passage through the shoal-lined Cape Hurd Channel. The wreck occurred in 1899.

The Wreck Today

The wreck of the John Walters is located in the shallow, narrow channel running between the south-west tip of Russel Island and a small barren island. All that remains is a 109-foot-long section of the hull bottom, the forward end of which is nosed into Russel Island. A small section of the starboard side, with chainplates, lies on top of the wreck. The two-foot by two-foot keelson runs the length of the wreck interrupted only by the centerboard box. The rudder of the John Walters lies on the bottom near the deep end of the wreck. A large section of the port side is located 80 feet west.

W. L. Wetmore

photo by Jack Youngblut

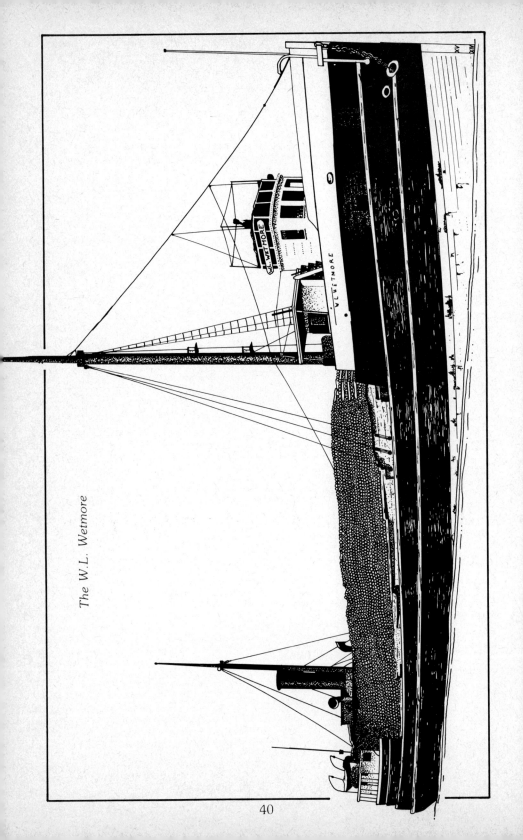

The W.L. Wetmore

W. L. Wetmore

Gross tonnage	— 819	Type —	Propeller steamer;
Length	— 214'		lumber hooker
Breadth	— 33'	Built —	Cleveland, Ohio 1871
Depth of hold	— 12'6"		by Quale & Martin

The Disaster

In the early hours of Nov. 29, 1901, the W.L. Wetmore with the schooners Brunette and James C. King in tow, entered the Devil Island Channel heading for Lake Huron. The holds and decks of all three vessels were loaded with Georgian Bay lumber. With visibility reduced by blowing snow and with heavy seas running out of the north-west, the procession ran aground on Russel Reef. At dawn's light, the Wetmore's crew abandoned ship and rowed to Tobermory in a lifeboat. The salvage tugs Metamora and Maguoila arrived the following day but only the Brunette could be salvaged.

The Wreck Today

The Wetmore is one of the best wrecks at Tobermory. It lies in 20 to 25 feet of water, just below Russel Island's west tip. Two mooring buoys are located to the south and west of the wreck.

The Wetmore lies in a south-east to north-west line with the stern to the south-west. It is here that you will find the massive oak rudder with its 15-foot blade and the sheared-off propeller, testimony of the Wetmore's first contact with the reef. The 25-foot-long drive shaft runs through the stern post to the engine mount (the steam engine was salvaged). You are now in the vicinity of one of the Wetmore's most awesome features — her boilers rise 12 feet above the wreckage. At the north-west end of the wreck there is a large length of anchor chain with the hawse pipes and one of the anchors nearby.* The port and starboard sides of the Wetmore have collapsed and now lie alongside the hull bottom. A section of railing still graces the port side and both sides have a large number of hanging knees attached. An interesting feature of these sides is the hooked scarph joints of the planking.

The massive construction of a wooden vessel such as the W. L. Wetmore deserves further investigation. The keelson is made up of six timbers, each, one-foot square. The frames measure five inches wide by 10 inches deep. Planking is three inches by 12 inches and all framing members and planking are of white oak.

---

* This anchor was part of the Orrie Vail collection of marine artifacts obtained by the Ministry of Natural Resources. It was returned to the site in 1984.

James C. King

Gross tonnage	— 512	Type — Three-masted schooner
Length	— 175'	Built — East Saginaw, Michigan
Breadth	— 33'	1867
Depth of hold	— 12'	by S.J. Tripp

The Disaster

As steam replaced sail, the schooners suffered a humiliating fate. They were loaded as barges and towed behind the steamers. Such was the demise of the large American schooner James C. King. For information concerning the wrecking of the King refer to the story of the W. L. Wetmore.

The Wreck Today

After she was driven onto Russel Reef, the King broke up and slid into deeper water. It now rests on a steep, rocky incline with the stern in 95 feet of water and the bow in 20 feet. The mooring buoy anchor is located near the bow with the rudder and steering gear nearby. As one swims deeper it will be observed that the hull has split along the keel and that the centerboard box has broken at the keel and lies atop the wreckage. Just forward of the centerboard box is an interesting feature called diagonal ceiling planking, used by some builders to add strength to the hull.

A large section of the King's starboard side and railing is located 200 feet west in 25 feet of water.

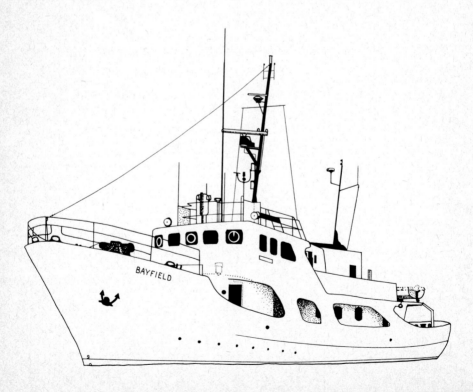

Philo Scoville

Gross tonnage	— 325	Type — schooner	
Length	— 139'	Built — Cleveland, Ohio	
Breadth	— 30'	1863	
Depth of hold	— 11'	by Quayle & Martin	

The Disaster

On Oct. 6, 1889 the Scoville was running light on Georgian Bay en route from Collingwood to Escanaba, Michigan. With a gale blowing from out of the northeast, conditions steadily deteriorated as she approached the Devil Island Channel. The Scoville drifted off course towards Russel Island and the anchors were dropped but they were dragged across the soft bottom and she went aground on the north shore of the island. Captain John O'Grady lost his life when he fell between the vessel and some rocks. The other four crewmen were rescued by a tug from Tobermory.

The Wreck Today

The wreck of the Philo Scoville rests on a steep incline in depths of between 55 and 95 feet. The mooring buoy anchor, in 95 feet, is located alongside the fallen bowsprit which leads to the intact bow section. The rest of the hull is broken into two main pieces, the bottom and the starboard side with railing. One of the anchors is in 90 feet of water, 150 feet to the east. The anchor chain runs from it towards shore, ending at the 30-foot depth. A section of the stern is lying in 35 feet of water, approximately 100 feet west of the main wreck.

The Griffon Cove Wreck

For many years it was believed the wreckage found in a shallow cove on Russel Island was that of the Griffon. Built near Niagara Falls in 1679 by French ship-wrights for the French explorer Sieur de La Salle, the Griffon was the first sailing vessel on the upper Great Lakes. Later the same year it left Green Bay on Lake Michigan manned by a crew of six and loaded with beaver pelts destined for Niagara Falls. The Griffon was never seen again.

In 1955 parts of a wrecked vessel were removed from the cove on the east end of Russel Island by Orrie Vail, a Tobermory fisherman, assisted by John MacLean, a newspaper reporter. Examination of the wreckage by marine historian Rowley Murphy, and C. H. J. Snider, a maritime artist, led to the conclusion that it was indeed wreckage from the Griffon. However, in 1956, Frank A. Meyers sent photos and all articles published about the Russel Island wreckage to the director of the Musee de la Marine in Paris and to an archaeologist specializing in French naval construction after the 16th century. They concluded that the wreckage "did not appear to be of French construction".

In 1977, after the death of Orrie Vail, the Ministry of Natural Resources acquired the wreckage. During the summers of 1978-79 further investigation of the Russel Island site was conducted by the staff of Fathom Five Provincial Park. Hundreds of artifacts were recovered including a padlock, identical to a lock included in the Orrie Vail collection. Both were detemined to have been manufactured between 1790 and 1830. Some of the ceramic pieces located at the wreck site bore the mark 'Barker & Son', a British firm producing only from 1850 to 1860.

Further study of the wreckage was carried out by Paul F. Hundley, a graduate student from the Institute of Nautical Archaeology, Texas A & M University. He constructed a model of the wreckage and from it developed a set of hull lines. The reconstruction of the wreckage taken from Russel Island produced a variation of a 'Mackinaw' boat, a type of vessel used extensively on Georgian Bay during the mid-1800's. Dimensions of the vessel wrecked were: length — 44'7 ", breadth — 14'7 ", depth of hull amidships — 3'5 ".

Tobermory fishermen aboard the tug David Marwick c. 1920

The Newaygo

Newaygo

Gross tonnage   — 906
Length   — 196'
Breadth   — 37'
Depth of hold   — 13'

Type — Propeller steamer;
      lumber hooker
Built — Marine City, Michigan
      1890

The Disaster

On Nov. 17, 1903, the Newaygo was attempting passage through the Devil Island Channel with the schooner Checotah in tow. Both vessels were laden with coal. Heavy seas and poor visibility due to snow caused the procession to run aground on the Northwest Bank. The crew and the schooner were rescued the following day by a tug from Tobermory. Attempts to remove the Newaygo failed and salvage operations were curtailed with the onset of an early winter. By spring, the ice-battered Newaygo had broken up and declared a total loss.

The Wreck Today

The wreck of the Newaygo rests in 15 to 25 feet of water along the south-east edge of the Northwest Bank. She is marked by a mooring buoy, the anchor of which is 40 feet south-east of the wreck. The largest piece of wreckage is the bottom of the hull which measures 160-feet-long by 16 feet wide. Between the mooring buoy anchor and the wreckage there is a section of the lower bow and a boiler measuring 10 feet long and five feet in diameter. These can be found 50 feet south of the main wreckage.

The Newaygo was a very heavily built vessel. Her construction details are worthy of attention during your dive. The keelson is made up of nine oak timbers, each measuring 12 inches by 14 inches. The frames measure 10 inches by 17 inches and are spaced only eight inches apart. Every second frame is further reinforced by an iron plate one-and-a-half inches thick.

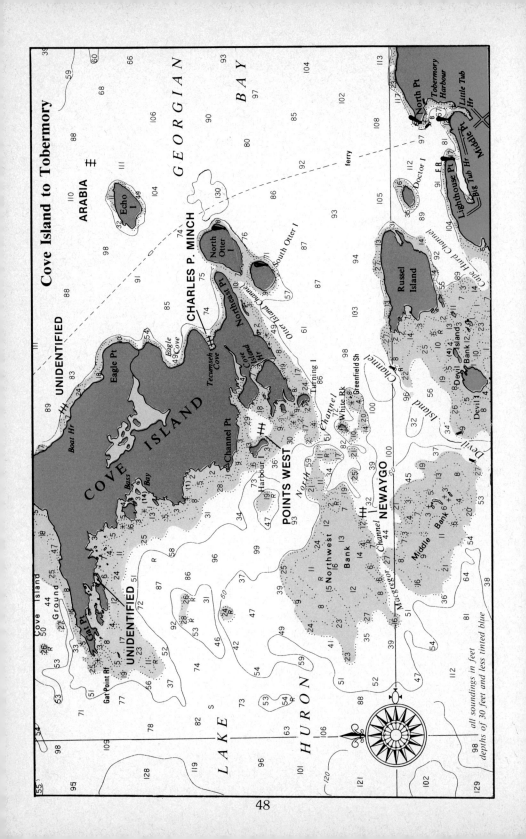

Cove Island to Tobermory

GEORGIAN BAY

LAKE HURON

COVE ISLAND

ARABIA

CHARLES P. MINCH

UNIDENTIFIED

POINTS WEST

NEWAYGO

Russel Island

Devil Island

North Otter I

South Otter I

Echo I

all soundings in feet
depths of 30 feet and less tinted blue

48

Largemouth Bass

Arabia

Gross tonnage	— 309	Type —	Three-masted barque
Length	— 131'	Built —	Kingston, Ontario
Breadth	— 26'		1853
Depth of hold	— 12'		by George Thurston

The Disaster

The Arabia was an aging vessel when she foundered off Echo Island on Oct. 4, 1884. She had been rebuilt three times during her long career and had run aground twice, once at Hay Island near Wiarton in 1881 and at Flowerpot Island in 1882.

On her last voyage, the Arabia was carrying 20,000 bushels of corn bound from Chicago to Midland, Ontario. Heavy seas were encountered on Lake Huron and the Arabia began to take on water and by the time Cove Island Lighthouse was passed the situation was grave. Water had overtaken the bilge pump and the crew was exhausted. Captain Henry Douville gave the order to lower the yawl boat and abandon ship. Shortly afterwards the Arabia slipped beneath the surface of Georgian Bay. The crew was rescued by the tug Clark.

The Wreck Today

The Arabia is a good wreck due to the fact that she foundered in open water, escaping the rocky shoreline that broke up many of the Tobermory wrecks. She rests in 120 feet of water, approximately 500 yards off the north-east corner of Echo Island. Two mooring buoys indicate its position and the buoy anchors are located about 30 feet east of the wreck. The Arabia lies along a north-south line with the bow to the north. The hull is intact with the exception of the main deck and transom which have collapsed. The bow of the Arabia is impressive with the jib-boom reaching out into the depths. The windlass, anchors, catheads and bilge-pump are all present.

Deadeyes, pulleys and pinrails are present along both sides but the masts that they once helped to secure have fallen. The foremast lies on the bottom near the starboard side, the mainmast has fallen forward over the port railing and the mizzenmast lies off the Arabia's port-quarter.

The Arabia's afterdeck has separated from the wreck and now rests against the starboard quarter. The steering gear and wheel lie alongside the afterdeck. *

Several interesting items found on the collapsed maindeck include the cookstove, centerboard windlass, capstan, spanker boom, and a yard with pulleys.

Due to its depth, low visibility and cold water temperatures, the Arabia is not suitable for inexperienced divers.

---

* On the 100th anniversary of the Arabia's loss, a team of divers from Wright State University placed a commemorative plaque next to the sterring wheel.

Wooden Windlass

1 Pawl-bitt
2 Carrick-bitts
3 Windlass-ends
4 Whelps
5 Strong-back
6 Crosshead
7 Purchase-rod
8 Pawl
9 Pawl-rim
10 Purchase-rims

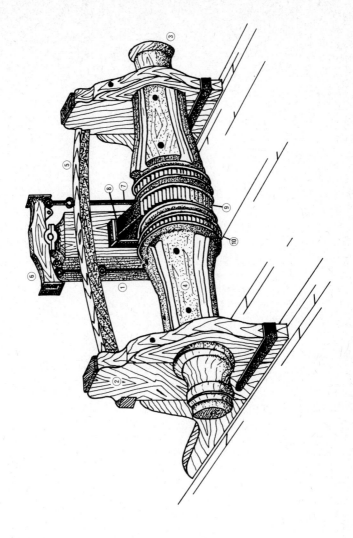

The Avalon Voyageur II — winter of 1981/82

photo by Jack Salen

The tour boat Blue Heron V along the Bruce Peninsula shoreline near Tobermory.

photo by Jack Salen

Charles P. Minch

Gross tonnage	— 408		Type	— Three-masted schooner
Length	— 154'		Built	— Vermillion, Ohio
Breadth	— 28'			1867
Depth of hold	— 12'			by Isaac W. Nicholas

The Disaster

In the early morning darkness of Oct. 26, 1898, the Charles P. Minch was anchored in the lee of Cove Island waiting for a strong south-west wind to subside. She was fully loaded with lumber destined for Chicago. The wind died but unfortunately started to blow with equal intensity from the opposite direction and the Minch was trapped. With anchors dragging, she was headed towards Cove Island's rocky shore. Captain William Kaufman ordered the yawl boat launched but it capsized and shortly afterwards the Minch ran aground at the entrance of Tecumseh Cove. The stranded crew tied a line to a large timber and threw it overboard. The breaking waves carried it ashore and the men pulled themselves to safety. They then made their way through the dense brush to Cove Island lighthouse.

The Wreck Today

The wreckage of the Charles P. Minch is located in two areas, both marked with mooring buoys. The main area of wreckage is along the south shore of Tecumseh Cove with several pieces of the vessel including centerboard box, the sides, the hull bottom and bow lying at the bottom of the rocky shoreline incline in depths of between 25 and 50 feet. There is also a rudder located west of the mooring buoy anchor. It is a small rudder and probably belongs to the schooner Tecumseh, wrecked in the same area in 1882.

The other area of wreckage is approximately 200 yards south of the cove. The mooring buoy anchor is in 60 feet of water and between it and the shore is a section of the Minch's side. A length of the keel and the rudder are located east of the buoy anchor. One of the Minch's anchors was recovered and is on display next to Little Tub Harbour.

The schooner Isabella Sands c. 1910

photo by Jack Youngblut

The boilers of the steamer W. L. Wetmore.

Lady Dufferin

Gross tonnage   — 385   Type — Schooner
Length   — 135'   Built — Port Burwell, Ontario

The Disaster

It was October 1886, and the Lady Dufferin was being towed from Cabot Head to Tobermory by the steamer W. B. Hall. The Dufferin was loaded with lumber from the schooner John Bentley, which had run aground at Cabot Head. As the pair made their way along the Bruce Peninsula's northern shoreline the north-easterly winds increased steadily and the heavy seas strained the tow line beyond its breaking point. The Hall made an attempt to retrieve the Dufferin but it was too late and the schooner was swept onto the rocks of what is now called Dufferin Point.

The Wreck Today

Dufferin Point is located one and a half miles east of Little Cove. The wreckage, situated just west of the point, is broken up and lies on the rocky incline in depths of between 40 and 100 feet.

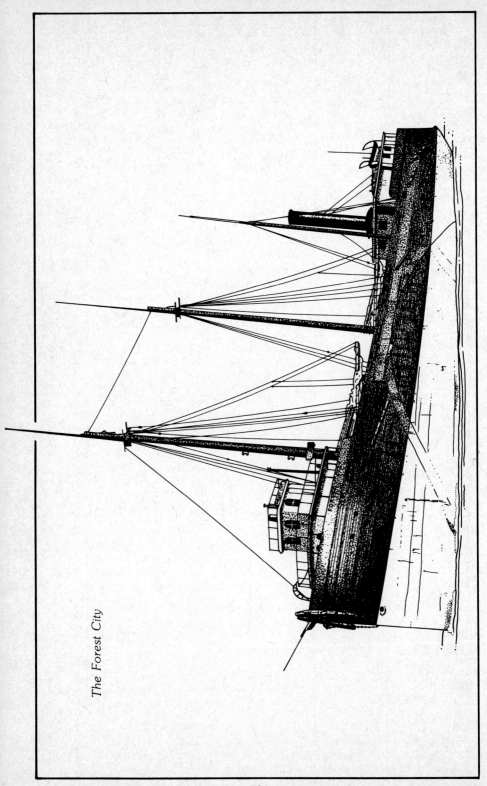

The Forest City

Forest City

Gross tonnage — 1236   Type — Propeller steamer
Length   — 216'   Built — Cleveland, Ohio
Breadth   — 32'   1870
Depth of hold   — 14'   by Peck & Masters

The Disaster

On June 5, 1904, heavy fog hung over the Tobermory Islands as the Forest City steamed towards Lake Huron. Her intended course was between Bear's Rump and Flowerpot but she had fallen off to starboard and as a result was stopped rather abruptly by Bear's Rump Island. The crew was taken off by the tug Joe Milton and the Forest City remained afloat for several weeks wedged into the rocks. Several unsuccessful attempts were made to dislodge her and eventually water seeping in through the damaged bow filled the hull and she slid off into deep water.

The Wreck Today

A piece of iron bow-plating from the Forest City, located along the north-east shoreline of Bear's Rump Island, indicates the point of impact. The wreck lies offshore on a very steep incline in depths of between 60 and 150 feet. The shallower forward section is broken up but the stern is intact. This wreck is suitable for experienced divers only.

Marion L. Breck

Gross tonnage	— 396	Type	— schooner
Length	— 127'	Re-built	— Kingston, Ontario
Breadth	— 23-1/2'		1863
Depth of hold	— 12'		by Calvin & Breck

The Disaster

The Marion L. Breck is one of the oldest vessels wrecked at Tobermory. She was originally built in 1840 and named the William Penn.

Early on Nov. 15, 1900, the Breck lost some of her canvas in gale-force winds. Unable to manoeuvre properly she ran aground on the south-east edge of Bear's Rump Shoal. At daybreak, with the seas washing over the deck, the Captain, his wife and the crew abandoned ship. They camped on Bear's Rump Island until rescued by Flowerpot lighthouse-keeper Dan Smith and his two sons.

The Wreck Today

The Breck is broken up and scattered over a large area. The largest piece of wreckage is a 40-foot-long section of the hull in 75 feet of water off the south-west tip of Bear's Rump Island. The capstan and one of the anchors are in 25 feet of water further south along the shoal's edge.

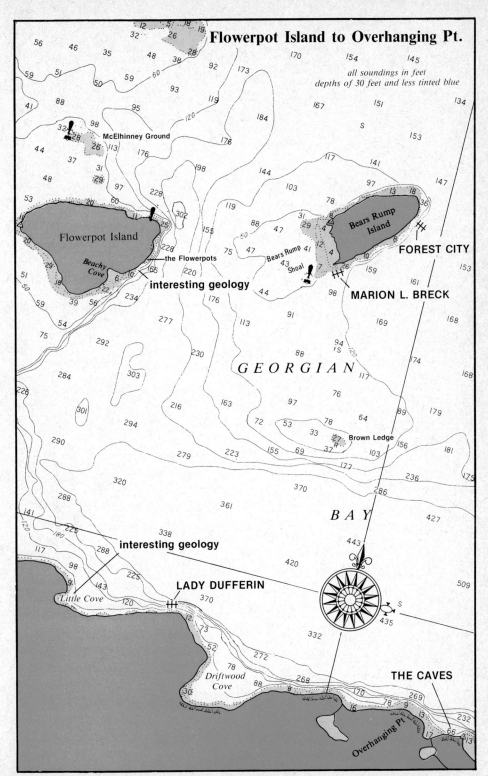

Flowerpot Island to Overhanging Pt.

all soundings in feet
depths of 30 feet and less tinted blue

McElhinney Ground

Flowerpot Island

Beachy Cove

the Flowerpots

interesting geology

Bears Rump Island

Bears Rump Shoal

FOREST CITY

MARION L. BRECK

GEORGIAN

Brown Ledge

BAY

interesting geology

LADY DUFFERIN

Little Cove

Driftwood Cove

THE CAVES

Overhanging Pt.

S

61

City of Cleveland

Gross tonnage	— 1609		Type — Propeller steamer
Length	— 255'		Built — Cleveland, Ohio
Breath	— 39'		1882
Depth of hold	— 18'		by Thomas Quayle & Son

The Disaster

The City of Cleveland was loaded at the Lake Superior port of Michipocoten with 2,300 tons of iron ore destined for Midland, Ontario. On Sept. 15, 1901 as she approached the entrance to Georgian Bay, the Cleveland was forced off-course by the monstrous seas of a south-west gale. The voyage ended as she hit the ledges west of Perserverance Island. The crew abandoned ship and rowed to Fitzwilliam Island.

The Wreck Today

The City of Cleveland is the largest and one of the most interesting wrecks near Tobermory. It is located some 800 yards north of the west end of Perserverance Island with the bow in 10 feet of water and the stern in 30 feet. The bottom of the hull is intact from bow to stern and the deck and sides have collapsed on top of it. The engine room is exposed and is the most interesting part of the wreck with the steam engine and massive boilers. The rudder and 12-foot propeller are located further aft. The cargo of iron ore is very much in evidence throughout the wreck area.

City of Cleveland

The steamer J. H. Jones at Tobermory c. 1905

Other Wrecks and Strandings in the Tobermory Area

ATHABASCA — This 270-foot Canadian Pacific steamer ran aground near Flowerpot Island lighthouse in October 1909. She was pulled off by three tugs and the steamer Alberta.

CASCADEN — On Oct. 15, 1871 the 138 gross-ton schooner was wrecked on the coastline above Cape Hurd. The wreckage is scattered over a large area.

CASTALIA — A 119-foot square-rigged brig, wrecked along the north-west shore of Cove Island in July, 1871.

D. R. MARTIN — A 137-foot schooner, aground and abandoned near Devil Island in November, 1904.

E. S. PEASE — steamer, aground near Devil Island 1904.

GOLDEN FISHER — 56-foot diesel fishing tug, burned near Cape Hurd, June 5, 1943.

GOLDEN WEST — 434 gross-ton schooner, wrecked at Snake Island Oct. 21, 1884.

JAMES G. WORTS -The Worts was being towed by the steamer City of Owen Sound when both vessels went aground near Devil Island in November 1885. The steamer was removed but the Worts went to pieces.

KENOSHA — steamer, aground on Bear's Rump Island November 1860. Pulled off by the steamer Ploughboy.

LILLY — schooner, wrecked at 'the entrance to Tobermory' September, 1852.

LOWELL — 345 gross-ton schooner, aground one-half mile west of Cove Island lighthouse September, 1871. Both of her anchors were lost. Pulled off by the tug Bob Anderson.

MARACAIBO — This 65-foot wooden yacht, built in 1933, caught fire in Big Tub Harbour in 1977. The engines and equipment were salvaged before she was towed to Little Cove and scuttled. No substantial pieces of wreckage have been located.

MARION EGAN — schooner aground near Cove Island light 1873. Pulled off by the tug Bob Anderson.

REGINA — 75-foot schooner foundered near Cove Island September 1881. Captain Amos Tripp drowned.

STARLIGHT — 307 gross-ton schooner aground near Eagle Point, Cove Island September, 1883. Removed that November by the tug Andrew J. Smith.

TECUMSEH — 111-foot schooner wrecked in Tecumseh Cove, Cove Island November 1882.

WH. H. MERRITT — 320 gross-ton schooner wrecked on Gig Point, Cove Island, 1865.

Underwater Geology of the Tobermory Area

The rock that makes up the Tobermory landscape above and below the surface is dolomite,* laid down 400 million years ago in a warm, shallow sea. Coral reefs flourished, growing upwards and expanding into dome shaped mounds called bioherms. Bear's Rump Island and each of the bluffs of Flowerpot Island are all ancient bioherms. They are also evident on a smaller scale along the Georgian Bay shoreline between Tobermory and Halfway Rock Point. Between the bioherms, layers of sediment built up into vast inter-reefal planes which have since hardened into what is called dolomite pavement. In some areas of the lake bed the pavement remains intact while in other places it has broken-off in layers into various sizes of rock pieces.

One million years ago climate in the northern latitudes began to deteriorate and the areas bioherms and dolomite pavement were scraped and scoured by four waves of glaciers, the last one beginning 13 thousand years ago. The dramatic results of a one-mile thick wall of ice advancing over the area are evident along the lake bottom. Striations in the dolomite pavement indicate that the glaciers travelled across this area from north-east to south-west. A few yards south of the wreck of the W. L. Wetmore is an area of larger glacial grooves, some of which are five feet deep and run for hundreds of feet. Glacial erratics, usually granite boulders carried to this area from the Canadian Shield, are common.

When the climate moderated about six thousand years ago, the melting glaciers retreated leaving vast glacial lakes behind, submerging the Bruce Peninsula. Since then, the lake levels have been dropping, forming flowerpots and sea caves in the process. The caves began to form as water percolated through fractures in the rock, dissolving out rounded passages. As the water level continued to drop the passages were enlarged by waves and freeze-thaw action. The caves just west of Halfway Rock Point are a fine illustration of the process.

Another geologic feature abundant in the Tobermory area is the pitting of the rock surface, giving it a swiss-cheese appearance. Underwater pitting is caused by the growth of algae which excretes acids that dissolve the pits.

*Dolomite is essentially limestone that contains higher levels of magnesium.

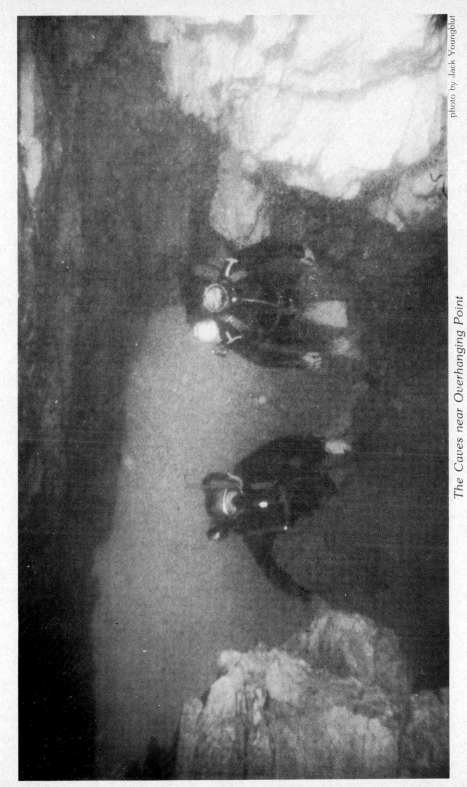

The Caves near Overhanging Point

Other Dive Sites in the Tobermory Area

ANCHOR — There is a large anchor of unknown origin in 60 feet of water along the shoreline between the ferry dock and Big Tub Harbour. It is located directly in front of the large, A-frame cottage.

FLOWERPOT ISLAND — The south-east shoreline of Flowerpot Island offers an impressive underwater landscape. The flat, shallow rock ledges plunge down a series of verticle faces to a maximum depth of 200 feet. Enter the water off-shore of the rain shelter located just east of the Beachy Cove boat docks. The Flowerpot Island tour boats cruise close to the shore in this area, necessitating the use of dive flags.

DUNK'S POINT — Located about one mile east of Tobermory, this area is very interesting for its underwater geology and landscape. An anchor is reported to be in 60 feet of water just north of the point.

LITTLE COVE — Locally known as Dave's Bay, this picturesque cove offers a variety of geological features. It is accessible by road and limited parking is available.

GAT POINT WRECK — A 60-foot-long section of hull framing and planking from an unidentified sailing vessel is located in less than 10 feet of water midway between Cove Island's Gat Point and Bass Bay.

CASSLE'S COVE WRECK — Below Cove Island lighthouse is a small inlet named Boat Harbour on the charts and known locally as Cassle's Cove, after Thomas Cassle who operated a lumber camp there from 1905 to 1910. The wreckage of an unidentified centerboard sailing vessel is located off-shore in depths of between 50 and 75 feet. A 90-foot-long section of the hull bottom lies in 70 feet of water and the sides and rudder lie in 50 feet. A decorative scalloped design is carved into the top of the rudder blade.

THE POINTS WEST — This 32-foot-long wooden guide boat, originally named the Flowerpot, was built in Tobermory in 1956 by Alf Carver. In Oct. 1984, it was scuttled in 50 feet of water, 300 feet east of Harbour Island. It lies intact on the sandy bottom.

THE CAVES — a good geologic dive. Located eight-and-one-half miles east of Tobermory, just beyond Overhanging Point in Indian Head Cove. The submerged passageways lead from Georgian Bay into a large, open-air chamber. Underwater lights are helpful. The preferred method of reaching this site is by boat although it can be reached by a one mile hike through Cyprus Lake Provincial Park.

The tug General in Little Tub Harbour c. 1915

Little Tub Harbour c. 1930

Glossary

AFT — at, near, or towards the stern of a vessel.

BACKSTAYS — a line slanting aft from the top of the mast down to the chain-plates at the vessel's side. They prevent the mast from inclining forwards or sideways.

BALLAST — additional weight placed low in a vessel's hull to increase stability.

BARQUE — a sailing vessel with its two forward masts square- rigged and its mizzen-mast fore and aft rigged.

BOOM — a spar extending the foot of a sail.

BOOM-SAIL — one in which the foot is extended on a boom and the head is usually on a gaff.

BOW — the front part of a vessel.

BOWSPRIT — a spar projecting beyond the bow to which the fore- topmast-stay is secured.

BREADTH — the distance from one side to the other at a vessel's widest point.

CAPSTAN — an apparatus used for hauling in docklines and lifting cargo.

CAT-HEAD — a square timber projecting beyond the bow, the outer end being fitted with block and tackle by which the anchor was lifted and secured aboard the vessel's bow.

CENTERBOARD — a retractable keel, housed in a watertight box extending from keel to deck. On a typical Great Lakes schooner the centerboard was 20 to 28 feet long, six to eight feet wide and approximately six inches thick. It was hinged forward and was raised or lowered by a deck-mounted winch located aft. When lowered the centerboard extended 10 to 15 feet below the hull. On some vessels the centerboard assembly is located along the centerline, thus interrupting the keel. Other builders preferred an offset centerboard, positioned next to the keel.

CROSS-HEAD — the metal fitting at the top of the rudder to which the steering gear is attached.

CEILING-PLANKING — planking attached to the inside of the vessel's frame.

CHAIN-PLATES — flat iron bars bolted to the vessel's sides to which the backstays and shrouds are secured.

DEAD-EYE — a flattened, circular piece of wood, perforated with holes through which which the lanyards are strung. Lanyards are short pieces of hemp, one end of which is fastened to the top of the chainplate and the other to the backstays or shrouds.

DEPTH of HOLD — the distance from the top of the ceiling planking to the bottom of the deck beams.

DRAUGHT-MARKS — the markings, in feet, carved into the bow-stem and stern-post indicating the depth of the submerged hull.

FORE-and-AFT-SCHOONER — a two or three-masted vessel with long lower-masts and short top-masts on which boom-sails and triangular gaff-topsails are carried.

FRAMES — transverse ribs forming the skeleton of a vessel.

GAFF — a spar having a jaw at one end that grasps the mast.

GAFF-SAIL — any sail in which the head is extended on a gaff.

GROSS-TONNAGE — the total capacity of the space within the hull and above-deck structures designed for the accommodation of cargo, stores, crew and passengers. In determining gross-tonnage 100 cubic feet equals one ton.

HAWSE PIPE — an iron fitting located in the upper bow through which the anchor chain passes.

HANGING-KNEES — timber brackets fitted under the deck and attached to the vessel's side.

HOOKED-SCARPH-JOINT — a method of joining pieces of lumber in which the end of each has been cut with a jagged pattern that meshes with the other. It was often used in the planking and railings of vessels.

JIB-BOOM — a spar attached to and extending beyond the bowsprit, to which the jib-stay was attached.

KEEL — the heavy timber running along the very bottom of the hull and extending from the bottom of the bow-stem to the bottom of the stern-post.

KEELSON — a timber, or timbers placed on top of the frames and directly above the keel and extending from bow-stern to stern- post. In a typical Great Lakes schooner the keelson was much heavier than the keel.

MACKINAW BOAT — a 25 to 45-foot-long, sharp-sterned, boom-sail rigged vessel developed by William Watts of Collingwood, Ontario. They were used extensively by the Georgian Bay fishermen of the mid-nineteenth century.

MAST-STEP — pieces of timber forming a bed for the foot of a mast.

MIZZENMAST — the aftermost mast in a three-masted vessel.

PIN-RAIL — a short length of wood fitted with belaying pins. The vessel's running gear was secured to the belaying pins.

PORT — the left side of a vessel.

PORT-QUARTER — the port side of the stern of a vessel.

RUDDER — the large wooden blade mounted on the stern-post which governs the direction of the vessel's movement.

SHROUD — a line supporting a mast.

SPANKER-BOOM — the spar extending aft from the mizzenmast of a barque, upon which the foot of the spanker sail is secured.

STARBOARD — the right side of a vessel.

STARBOARD-QUARTER — the starboard side of the stern of a vessel.

STEM — the timber forming the fore part of the hull, extending from the keel to bowsprit.

STERN — the after part of a vessel.

STERN-POST — the heavy timber extending vertically from the after end of the keel to the upper-deck. The rudder was hinged on the stern-post.

STERN-TUBE — a metal tube extending from the stuffing box through the stern-post of a propeller-driven vessel. The propeller shaft runs inside of the stern-tube.

TOPSAIL-SCHOONER — a vessel with the foremast fitted with yards and square sails. The other mast or masts have long lower-masts and short top-masts on which boom-sails and triangular gaff topsails are carried.

WINDLASS — a large winch mounted transversly on the fore-deck used to haul up the anchors.

YARD — a spar tapered at the ends, secured in the middle to a mast and on which the head of a square sail was suspended.

Little Tub Harbour c. 1915

Bibliography

Amos, Art and Patrick Folkes, *A Diver's Guide to Georgian Bay*, 1979.
Barry, James, *Georgian Bay, the Sixth Great Lake*, Toronto, 1968.
Folkes, Patrick, *Shipwrecks of the Saugeen, 1828 - 1938*, 1970.
McKenzie, Ruth, *Admiral Bayfield, Pioneer Nautical Surveyor*, Ottawa, 1976.
Paasch, Capt. H., *Illustrated Marine Encyclopedia*, Watford, England, 1890.

Other Sources of Information

Hundley, Paul F., *The Griffon Cove Wreck, a case study in archaeological reconstruction of timber hull remains.*
Cowell, D.W., *Karst Geomorphology of the Northern Bruce Peninsula*, 1974.
McClellan, Stan, *The Griffon Cove Project, a preliminary archaelogical investigation, 1978, and 1979 field season supplement.*
Nautical Charts 2201, 2235 and 2274, published by the Canadian Hydrographic Service, Ottawa.

Published by the Mariner Chart Shop

Tobermory Shipwreck Chart
Great Lakes Shipwreck Chart
Vancouver Island Shipwreck Chart
Southern Georgian Bay Shipwreck Chart
Sea Disasters — a shipwreck chart of the world.
Lake Ships — a wall chart of Great Lakes vessels
Fishing Vessels of the World — a wall chart of commercial fishing vessels
Famous Sail — a wall chart of famous sailing ships
Manitoulin Island — a decorative map
The Northern Bruce — a decorative map of the Bruce Peninsula
The Bruce — a guide to the Bruce Peninsula by Lindsey Brown

For more information write to:
The Mariner Chart Shop
Box 9
Tobermory, Ontario
N0H 2R0

Dive Log

Date	Site	Bottom Time	Comments

Dive Log

Date	Site	Bottom Time	Comments

Index to the Shipwrecks